How To Find Your Soulmate

Effective Strategies For Cultivating A Meaningful And Sustaining Romantic Partnership

(Strategies For Discovering Your Ideal Life Partner And Cultivating A Longstanding Bond)

Francisco Donnelly

TABLE OF CONTENT

Introduction 1

The Narrative Of Discovering My True Life Partner
....26

Getting To Know Him 38

The Process Of Identifying An Ideal Life Partner ...52

Select A Website, Establish Your Profile, And Determine Your Specific Preferences. 62

Get Away From Me! 87

From Friendship To Love 136

Introduction

Soulmate. At a certain point in the past, we pondered whether we would eventually encounter our respective destinies. We inquire whether the individual we are currently in the company of is indeed the one destined for us. There exists a plethora of accounts regarding individuals discovering their ideal partner, their perfect counterpart, their soulmate, which can occasionally seem exceedingly miraculous to comprehend, yet our faith in such occurrences persists. Indeed, love operates in enigmatic manners. If you are seeking to ascertain its feasibility, it indeed is. It is possible to discover one's soulmate.

Soulmates are commonly thought to be our 'perfect romantic match', the complementary counterpart of our inner being. If you experience instances of yearning and longing, it is likely due to the fact that you have not yet encountered the person who possesses the ability to alleviate your feelings of loneliness. If you possess anxieties, he certainly possesses techniques to alleviate them. He has the capacity to alleviate your hesitation; he embodies joy. Soulmates serve to enhance our lives, rather than serving as our sole source of fulfillment.

The initial indication in determining if he is the suitable individual is when both your heart and mind firmly convey that he indeed is. You will possess the knowledge, irrespective of your familiarity with the mechanics. That is the delight that soulmates bestow upon all individuals.

Contemplating the existence of a compatible soul for each of us is a profoundly beautiful notion. The universe is of such immense proportions that the quest for our soulmates assumes the character of an awe-inspiring odyssey. The notion appears enigmatic, yet it compellingly tugs at the depths of our emotions. It instills within us a compelling motivation to rise and greet each day, driven by the fervent aspiration that we may fortuitously encounter them. The situation can become truly gratifying, given the imperfect nature of our world, discovering one's soulmate during the most unexpected moments is arguably the most exquisite experience that can befall any individual.

Therefore, the query at hand is how to locate one's soulmate amidst a lack of initial prospects and a dearth of indications as to whom to seek out. It merely requires confirmation and conscientiousness, whereby, at an opportune moment, you shall be capable of recognizing the singular individual.

Finding Your Soulmate

Are you interested in discovering your soulmate? Are you weary and exhausted from your inability to determine a suitable course of action? Discovering your life partner is straightforward. With accurate knowledge at your disposal, you will embark upon the path to experiencing the emotion of love. You will become the subject of admiration among your peers. There exist uncomplicated yet remarkably efficient measures entailed. If you adhere to these steps derived directly from counseling techniques, your success will be guaranteed. Prior to the disclosure of the procedural instructions, it is imperative that you possess a comprehensive understanding of the advantages and verifiable information regarding a soulmate love relationship.

Scientific Evidence: As per the research conducted by psychologist Abraham Maslow, every human action can be attributed to one or more essential needs.

The primary requirement is social in nature.

Individuals require love, affection, compassion, and acceptance. They are the aspects most coveted by many individuals in their romantic relationships. One of the motives prompting individuals to seek their soulmate is the desire for genuine love, affection, and acceptance. It is probable that you have experienced a romantic involvement or relationship in which you believed your desires were being fulfilled, only to be disappointed and undergo an emotional setback, resulting in heartbreak. Because these needs are a driving force in your life, you continue to search, believing in love just as many people do. If your soulmate has not yet arrived, do not allow that to be a cause for concern. You are not alone.

The second requirement pertains to the aspect of esteem.

This represents the fundamental human necessity for accomplishment, attention, acknowledgement, and esteem. Soulmate connections have been recognized for their ability to elevate one's self-confidence. Soulmates afford each other the proper level of attention they merit. They mutually acknowledge each other as alliance members and possess a remarkable level of reverence for one another, regardless of their socioeconomic statuses. Soulmate love is characterized by its unconditional nature, a quality that is exceptionally rare. In actuality, a scientific finding has indicated that canines exhibit unwavering affection towards their human caregivers. As individuals, often we anticipate certain expectations from the opposite gender before we believe we can develop affection towards that individual. You are an individual capable of experiencing emotions; it is your rightful entitlement to experience unconditional affection with your compatible life partner.

Essential Components Required at Present

For countless women, the process of dating can be perceived as monotonous since more often than not, they fail to encounter the suitable individual. If you find yourself trapped in a repetitive cycle and desire to discover your soulmate, it is essential to explore certain key components that are instrumental in captivating the emotions and essence of a respectable gentleman. The subsequent information will assist you in locating that individual and maximizing your available opportunities. Make sure that you employ a variety of different tactics to wrangle in someone that is worthwhile; otherwise you could be once again stuck in the same old cycle.

Confidence

The majority of individuals fail to comprehend the true extent of confidence's immense power. If you are able to cultivate a sufficient amount of self-esteem to possess confidence in general, you will possess a formidable asset in your favor. You will discover that this aspect holds significant importance in your life, particularly when it pertains to identifying the ideal partner. Confidence possesses such immense strength that it has the potential to enable one to discover someone at an accelerated rate. Strive to ascertain a more definitive approach and refrain from hasty resolutions, as this is not an instantaneous occurrence.

Culture

In order to find a suitable partner, it is important to possess a refined level of cultural knowledge and social sophistication. Engage in the pursuit of discovering the aesthetically pleasing aspects present within your urban locality, traverse your immediate environment, partake in visits to reputable art institutions, and derive pleasure from the experiences commonly overlooked by others. You are not required to undertake all of these tasks simultaneously, but it is advisable to allocate some personal time and persist in gaining knowledge. You will discover that engaging in this activity is genuinely distinctive, and through this experience, you will embark on a journey of self-discovery, explore your preferences, and encounter a diverse array of remarkable individuals. Do not neglect or overlook this opportunity, as many individuals simply adhere to their usual routines and rely on chance for someone to discover them.

Adventure

This statement is not an invitation to visit nightclubs and engage in excessive drinking throughout the night, but rather an encouragement to contemplate the possibility of engaging in solitary activities and deriving enjoyment from them. One may struggle to find a suitable male companion if they consistently maintain a low profile. However, if one frequently ventures into public spaces and visibly indulges in personal activities, they are likely to attract the attention of eligible bachelors who are similarly engaged in such pursuits. This factor is of utmost significance that you would want to utilize in your endeavor to discover your soulmate.

Regardless of your actions, it is imperative that you refrain from becoming despondent and remain indoors during the morning. This is the worst thing that you can do as it will only fuel depression and that will not get you the right man. On the contrary, resist the idea of experiencing sadness or desperation, and choose to engage in activities that bring you happiness. If it entails experiencing the natural environment, proceed and engage in it. You will realize that there is a profound sense of liberation in life when one embraces it to the utmost extent. Proceed, observe what lies beyond and inevitably you shall acquire your one true companion in due time.

Manifesting Magic: Part Three

Section three of The Art of Happiness, Peace & Purpose delves into our interpersonal relationships. The objective of this book is to substantially enhance the love, harmony, and camaraderie permeating your life. A person of significant financial means who has strained relationships cannot be regarded as truly successful and is unlikely to experience genuine happiness. During the upcoming hour, I will hereby disclose the intricate nuances involved in establishing and nurturing profound connections that exude an aura of enchantment.

I am composing this portion of the book at an altitude of 34,000 feet above the state of Texas, while en route to San Francisco on a flight. As I observe the diverse array of individuals occupying this aircraft cabin, I am prompted to acknowledge my limited familiarity with you, the discerning reader of this literary work. Certainly, I understand that you have an earnest desire to enhance specific facets of your life and that you are willing to allocate your resources, both time and financial, towards attaining that objective. Furthermore, it would be unreasonable to assume that I possess any additional information about you. I am uncertain about your gender. Nevertheless, there is one thing of which I am undoubtedly convinced -

there exists a fractured relationship in your current circumstances. This could be exemplified by the presence of friction in professional relationships with your supervisor, in personal relationships with your partner, sibling, or even by harboring unresolved resentment towards one or both of your parents.

I offer my perspective on this matter based on personal encounters, as I endured numerous years perceiving a sense of antagonism from the world around me. My employer exhibited disrespectful behavior, the individuals with whom I collaborated manifested a lack of competence while being unjustly compensated, and I experienced disappointment from my dear ones to some extent. I held a firm conviction that placing my trust solely in myself was imperative, for any alternative would prove to be nothing short of foolishness. Following the eventual breakdown of my marriage in 2011, I embarked on a prolonged succession of brief interpersonal connections of a romantic nature. Every instance was characterized by both drama and trauma, culminating in a subsequent and acrimonious separation.

After every unsuccessful endeavor to discover my ideal companion, I would assert that the latest unsuccessful partnership was destined for failure from the outset due to her perceived mental instability, excessive emotional dependence, possessiveness, lack of empathy, or any other assortment of reasons that justified her inability to provide me with the affectionate relationship I yearned for.

I hope by now you know that I never write from atop an ivory tower. I am not among those individuals considered as "spiritual gurus" who disapprovingly shake their heads and utter "tut, tut, tut - cease your current way of living and commence emulating my own." Regrettably, I impart the knowledge I have acquired through personal adversity and the difficult lessons I have endured in my literary works.

Kindly undertake a task on my behalf and reflect upon the interpersonal connection in your life that you perceive as being fractured or impaired. A relationship that brings about significant discomfort, despite your strong desire for it to be a source of love and positivity in your life. Regardless of the underlying cause you believe to be the crux of the issue, I must assert that the actual origin of the problem is significantly distant from your current perception. Regardless of whether you perceive this individual as arrogant, unpleasant, patronizing, or simply self-centered, the designation you assign is merely a fallacy.

The compatibility of my professional association with my superior, Brian (name altered), was hindered due to his lack of diligence and incompetence, which consequently led to a dearth of admiration from my end. My relationship with Sarah was never going to work because she didn't really care what I wanted out of life, only what she wanted. The relationship between Catherine and myself failed to materialize due to her substantial levels of insecurity and neediness.

The aforementioned justifications for the lack of success in my life are mere illusions, which I once ardently subscribed to. I employed them as a means of safeguarding my self-image, unequivocally declining to acknowledge accountability for the pervasive lack of harmony in my life. The fact of the matter is as follows: Brian was not any lazier than I was. Sarah was equally committed to her own life, and my characterization of Catherine as insecure could be likened to a fashion model accusing her colleague of excessive vanity.

In the forthcoming segment, Manifesting Magic Part 3, I will enlighten you on the clandestine method of effectively cultivating profoundly captivating relationships within your existence.

Whether these are professional, personal or even close family. We are embarking upon a transformative voyage, commencing at the very root of all conflicts – yourself. Regardless of your willingness to acknowledge it, I am here to assert that the genesis of all the turbulent relationships in your life lies within you.

If one examines the situation from a rational standpoint, it becomes evident that one's supervisor cannot truly be categorised as disagreeable, as such a judgment would necessitate unanimous consensus. However, I believe you are cognizant of individuals who genuinely hold a positive view towards him, albeit necessitating exploration beyond the confines of the professional setting and extending to his circle of acquaintances and loved ones. The accurate designation in this situation would be 'your superior is exhibiting unpleasant behavior towards you'. This course prompts the highly logical inquiry as to his existence.

In Manifesting Magic Part 3, I shall elucidate the precise reasons behind your distinct selection for such inequitable treatment, and, more significantly, I shall illuminate the means by which you can put an end to its perpetuation.

We have collectively misconstrued the concept of labelling. We perceive the issue within our fractured relationships as disagreements in the other individual that have progressively become more incongruent with our own operational methodology. The difficult lesson to grasp is that the issues you encounter in others are simply manifestations of the issues inherent within yourself. What I am attempting to articulate is that the disharmony was never inherent in Brian, Sarah, or Catherine, but rather originated within myself from the outset. My relationships served as a reflection of the inner anguish within me.

At this nascent stage of the book, I firmly anticipate the likelihood of losing a substantial segment of my readership. Based on the severity of the relationship you are contemplating, as well as the utterly unacceptable experiences they may have subjected you to. I empathize entirely with your indignation and affront towards the mere insinuation that you bear any responsibility for their reprehensible conduct.

Thus, you are presented with an opportunity to make a decision. One could choose to convey their anger and discontent by articulating strong criticism regarding the book in various public forums, while refraining from engaging with its pristine pages any further. Additionally, it would be advisable to persist in repairing the fractured romantic connection or potentially explore alternative relationships." May I present an alternative perspective, attempting to convince you to consider taking a calculated risk, wherein I have personally accepted and reconciled with this unpleasant reality, discovering that its therapeutic qualities effectively alleviate the suffering of those affected.

Based on my definite knowledge, I can assure you that by persisting alongside me in this endeavor and faithfully applying the challenging conceptual changes I am about to propose, your existence will be elevated and augmented far beyond what you can presently conceive.

The Narrative Of Discovering My True Life Partner

Surprisingly, I found my soulmate in a rather unforeseen manner. As previously indicated, I was not actively seeking a partner during that specific period, as I had recently terminated my engagement. Although I experienced emotional distress for a period of time, upon reflection, I have come to realize that it was, in fact, a fortuitous turn of events. Thus, I must admit that I was not prepared to embark upon a new romantic endeavor.

I had been engaged in volunteer activities for a non-profit organization that had established centers throughout the midwestern region. In 1993, I relocated to St. Louis in the capacity of a director for one of these centers. During a weekend, I had the opportunity to engage in conversation with the director of the Springfield, Missouri school affiliated with this organization whilst at its headquarters.

The director inquired whether I would consider exchanging positions with him, in which I would relocate to Springfield while he would transfer to St. Louis. After reflecting on this matter for approximately half a minute, I promptly responded with an unequivocal affirmation.

It was difficult for me to fathom. I had earnestly contemplated the prospect of relocating to a different city without securing employment beforehand, yet I perceived it as a decision of paramount importance that I could not evade. It was a significant act of trust to determine my relocation, yet fortunately, I had several months' time until the actual transition.

I arrived in Springfield on the 1st of August, carrying the final remnants of my belongings within my vehicle. Subsequently, it appeared as though cosmic forces were aligned to facilitate the discovery of my kindred spirit.

Once I had completed the task of unpacking all my belongings, I proceeded to engage in a conversation with the director of the educational institution with whom I was participating in a program exchange, in order to be appropriately acquainted with the ongoing affairs at the facility. During our conversation, he informed me that an additional responsibility would be assigned to me: I would have the opportunity to serve as the host of a local cable TV program, which would entail the task of sourcing and interviewing guests. To say that this caught me off guard would be an understatement, yet I couldn't help but feel intrigued by the prospects of this endeavor.

Curiously, I had envisioned myself engaged in a similar endeavor, and fortuitously, an opportunity has arisen. Shortly after relocating to Springfield, an individual hailing from California telephoned the center. He delivered a formal address in the city of Springfield pertaining to the activities and endeavors of the educational institution. Our initial conversation was so engaging that I proposed meeting in person for dinner to further our discussion.

During the dinner, I informed him that I was the host of a local cable TV program and inquired if he would be interested in appearing as my inaugural guest. Unbeknownst to me, he had already encountered the person who would later become my soulmate and future spouse. That knowledge came later. The television program was a success with this gentleman as my esteemed guest. However, the moment had arrived to search for my next guest.

I opted to visit a nearby establishment specializing in metaphysical literature in order to ascertain the availability of informative pamphlets or leaflets that could assist me in locating a suitable guest. After reaching the bookstore, I discovered a multitude of brochures and business cards belonging to individuals who possess the potential to become valuable guests for the show. I was particularly drawn to one specific brochure. It was the possession of a woman who engaged in a distinctive procedure that had piqued my curiosity (and no, it was not owned by my destined life partner, but instead her doppelgänger, Linda!).

Consequently, I contacted Linda and informed her regarding the television program. Upon making a formal request to access a video recording of the program, she subsequently consented to being invited as a guest. Subsequently, we scheduled a meeting to convene and deliberate upon the topics that we would address during the program.

Several days later, I encountered Linda at her establishment where she presided over a tailoring shop, in order to deliberate on the forthcoming event. I engaged in a brief conversation with her, following which she promptly vacated the premises. Subsequently, without prior expectation, her identical twin, distinguished by her platinum blond hair, engaged me in conversation regarding a subject she deemed compelling for the broadcast. She provided me with her explanation for approximately two minutes before abruptly leaving. I pondered, "What was the purpose of that encounter?" Subsequently, I bestowed upon my significant other the nickname "the hit and run blonde," as it accurately described the fleeting nature of our interaction. I initially believed I had command over the situation, but it is plausible that cosmic forces were at play, leading to a certain outcome.

Shortly thereafter, the individual from the state of California whom I had conversed with telephonically subsequent to my relocation to Springfield, entered the premises. I found it difficult to comprehend! What a seemingly minuscule world we inhabited! My acquaintance had only recently encountered these two women, and to my astonishment, there he stood at the entrance! As it transpired, he intended to partake in our evening repast.

While dining, I engaged in a discussion with Linda regarding the topics we wished to address during the upcoming presentation. Subsequently, my acquaintance from California proposed, "Why not invite Brenda to participate in the show as well?" I distinctly recollect deliberating over this suggestion and contemplating whether it was feasible for me to do so. However, after pondering the idea, I arrived at the conclusion that there was no reason not to proceed. Consequently, rather than featuring a solitary guest on the upcoming show, I made the decision to invite the twins, Linda and Brenda, to participate instead. At this juncture, I must admit that I had some reservations regarding the potential challenges that lay ahead of me. It should be noted that there was no immediate sentimental connection upon my initial encounter with Brenda.

It is worth mentioning that Brenda and Linda had planned to conduct a four-week workshop on a subject that I had been fervently interested in for the preceding few years before our encounter. Indeed, I was astounded when Linda informed me that they were instructing this exceedingly esoteric subject matter in which I held a keen interest. What were the likelihood or probability of that occurrence? I am doing quite well, as you will come to realize in due course. Given my busy teaching schedule, I was hoping to allocate an evening to be able to participate in at least one of the workshops.

The performance featuring the twins was highly successful. After conversing with Brenda, it has been determined that

I will feature her exclusively in my upcoming show.

Brenda and I have made a joint decision to convene for dinner prior to the show, with the purpose of deliberating upon the topics that will be discussed. During our dinner engagement, we engaged in an uninterrupted conversation for a duration of two hours, almost neglecting to address the imminent show. Fortunately, Brenda had graciously prepared a set of inquiries that I could pose to her during the imminent broadcast. That proved to be incredibly beneficial and deserving of immense gratitude.

We derived immense pleasure from one another's company. Upon my departure, I made the suggestion that we should arrange another dinner gathering in the future. Due to my significant workload at the school, it would take a number of weeks before that could occur. I encountered Brenda for the following instance during one of their workshops, which took place several weeks later.

At long last, the evening had arrived for me to partake in the twins' seminar. I was really excited. The workshop was really interesting. I had the privilege of being selected as a participant for an exercise during the workshop, which I thoroughly enjoyed. Following the conclusion of the workshop, I lingered in the vicinity. I inquired of Brenda whether she would be interested in arranging a meeting for dinner at a convenient time. She said, "Yes!"

A week later, we had our initial meeting, in a manner of speaking. It truly seemed as though we were already acquainted and simply relishing each other's company, almost more akin to a friendly encounter rather than a romantic outing. I can assure you that I had no ulterior motive and was allowing events to progress in an organic manner. I did not have any intention of pursuing a romantic relationship. I experienced a mild sense of caution following the conclusion of my previous romantic partnership.

Notably, Brenda had recently concluded a dissatisfying marriage of 26 years, prompting her relocation from San Antonio to Springfield in order to reside alongside her identical twin sister, Linda. Therefore, she was not particularly prepared to embark on another romantic commitment once more.

However, we commenced a regular cadence of rendezvous, approximately once per week, simply relishing each other's companionship. We shared common interests. It appeared that we shared a mutual understanding right from the outset. Our relationship evolved naturally. Approximately eighteen months later, we entered into matrimony. I am deeply grateful each day for the presence of Brenda in my life. We share a deep resonance on multiple planes. I firmly believe that I have discovered my soulmate.

Getting To Know Him

""Indeed! Another victory!" The fair-haired university senior, an attractive individual named Jay, clasped his hands together in jubilation.

Carrie and I made eye contact. He was cheating. Again.

Daniela, positioned opposite me, directed her gaze towards Jay, her brow subtly elevated. It appears that you have omitted certain words from the card.

Jay's victorious smile faded. Indeed, I was in proximity. You consistently prevent me from attaining respite."

Optimal enjoyment of the game is ensured when all individuals adhere to the prescribed regulations.

Now Jay frowned. I intend to acquire additional chips." He stood up from the floor and proceeded to make his way into the kitchen.

Carrie discreetly expressed her astonishment, murmuring, whilst glancing at the remaining four participants gathered around the game board.

Shannon nodded. This marks the third occurrence of a game night within a span of two months, during which he has been found guilty of cheating consistently.

In the span of two months since Carrie had convinced me to become a member of this local young adult events group, I have experienced unparalleled levels of enjoyment. Adjacent to Dan was a modest and demure individual, recently graduated from university, demonstrating an exceptional ability to passionately perform in front of a diverse crowd. Shannon had recently graduated from high school and occasionally exhibited a sharp wit, but was establishing herself as a dependable companion. Last weekend, she generously lent me ten dollars for gasoline when I inadvertently left my purse behind, insisting it was a gesture of goodwill.

Dan, a twenty-one-year-old apprentice in his father's landscaping business, displayed impeccable manners towards the female members of our group. Furthermore, he possessed a remarkable sense of humor and appeared to possess a level of integrity and maturity unparalleled among my male acquaintances younger than thirty years old.

I was starting to develop a positive sentiment towards him.

"Let us redirect our attention to the favorable aspects, ladies." Dan's gaze shifted towards me, prompting an involuntary response as I reciprocated his smile.

"I'm game," I agreed. Furthermore, should we continue speaking in hushed tones...

Dan nodded. In a regular speaking tone, he inquired, "Who among us is interested in participating in a vocal competition?" Eighties music only?"

Jay reentered the room carrying a platter of chips, however, he chose to join the alternate group engaged in gaming. Without acknowledging the events that transpired within our group, he proceeded to engage in lighthearted banter with the female members of the adjacent group.

I found it necessary to concur with Carrie. He was a jerk. In an intriguing turn of events, had he solicited a romantic outing with me a mere two months earlier, I would have readily acquiesced. She exhibited an excellent notion by engaging in the opportunity to familiarize herself with various gentlemen within a collective environment.

***

In the preceding chapter, I elucidated the concept of purposeful engagement in the act of waiting, wherein one refrains from exerting influence over the ultimate outcome of the awaited event, specifically in the context of finding one's soul mate. However, due to the pervasive influence of contemporary Western culture, your ability to identify your soulmate may be challenged should you abstain from engaging in dating activities.

This chapter will provide you with a demonstration of the process. However, before I proceed, I must first acknowledge a matter of importance: indeed, the occurrence of love at first sight is feasible. One could potentially encounter an individual, experience an immediate connection, proceed to wed the following day, and subsequently lead a blissful lifelong partnership. That could potentially occur in your situation.

But will it? How probable is it? In all likelihood, it is unlikely to be the case. Many individuals require additional time and exertion in the pursuit of their ideal life partner. You could potentially belong to the minority of individuals who fall into this category. However, the subsequent details are provided as a precautionary measure if you are not already aware.

The checklist

Throughout the course of this book, I have subtly alluded on multiple occasions to specific attributes that one should consider when selecting a prospective life partner. In the literary work titled 'Date...Or Soul mate?' Neil Clark Warren advises individuals to create two distinct lists, one outlining essential qualities and attributes they seek in a lifelong companion, and the other enumerating traits or behaviors that they find intolerable in a potential partner.

Warren further suggests that it is advisable for each list to comprise a total of ten items. Moreover, exceeding that threshold suggests an excessive idealism and diminishes the likelihood of encountering a compatible life partner in the future. With a smaller quantity, it is possible that your level of selectiveness is insufficient.

I discovered this methodology to be immensely beneficial during my emotional recovery and subsequent search for a compatible life partner; hence, I kindly impart it to you. Please feel free to allocate whatever amount of time is necessary for the compilation of the lists. Consider the factors that hold significance in your life, such as your long-term objectives and the criteria necessary in a partner to instill a sense of safety and stability.

Please find enclosed the compiled lists I have prepared:

Must have

Passion for Jesus

Financial wisdom

Moderately balanced in terms of introversion and extroversion, meaning not excessively inclined towards either end of the spectrum.

Intelligent conversationalist

Takes care of self

Enjoys outdoor leisurely activities

Consistency between words and deeds

Galatians 5: 22-23 enumerates the virtues encapsulated by the Spirit.

Affectionate

Embraces and supports my holistic approach to health

Can't stand

Any form of dependency, including sports and television.

Not teachable

Procrastinator

Controlling/domineering

Psychologically unpredictable (including the inability to manage anger)

Materialistic

Lazy

Critical/judgmental of others

Do I have any adult children who are less than twelve years younger than me?

I have included this final item on the list due to the fact that a couple of months prior to compiling these lists, the individual whom I previously referred to and had feelings for, unexpectedly revealed that he is the father of a sixteen-year-old daughter.

Coincidentally, he wound up accompanying me down the aisle during the wedding ceremony between Jerry and me. Go figure.

Ideally, it is recommended that your list is derived from your personal life encounters thus far, with the exclusion of singling out any particular individual. Similar to my situation, the individual whom you currently have under consideration may ultimately prove to be unsuitable for you.

By this point, you might be curious about the outcome of my inventory. Allow me to rephrase that in a formal tone: "Allow me to express it in a different manner: in the months preceding our wedding, I harbored the conviction that Jerry possessed all the essential qualities I sought, while lacking any objectionable traits. However, it is important to acknowledge, my dear friend, that both you and your intended spouse tend to present your most favorable selves prior to marriage." After entering into matrimony, you will both exhibit authentic behavior and come to realize that he does not quite align with the predetermined set of criteria. However, he will soon come to realize that you are not quite the flawless princess he envisioned when he entered into matrimony with you.

Still, make the lists. Jerry possesses the majority of those qualities on a frequent basis, albeit their manifestation may deviate from my initial preconceived notions prior to our encounter. Possessing a comprehensive understanding of the attributes you desire to find, as well as those you wish to avert, in a spouse, will greatly contribute to maximizing the potential for marital bliss in your life.

Once you have compiled your lists, you can proceed to actively promote yourself in the public domain. Be mindful that your objective is not to actively pursue an ideal partner, but rather to navigate life in a manner that will naturally attract him to you, thus sparing you from any further emotional distress.

Dance classes

I have accorded this organization the top position on my list of social affiliations due to the fact that it is where Jerry and I first crossed paths. Recall that individual towards whom I previously harbored romantic feelings? He possessed exceptional skills in Country-Western dancing, and my initial motivation to begin taking lessons stemmed from a desire to leave a lasting impression on him.

Upon realizing his complete lack of reciprocation of my emotions, I resolved to persist in attending dance classes due to my newfound appreciation for engaging in a socially-oriented activity beyond the confines of my religious community. And – to be completely honest – I longed for the tactile connection that was absent from my life as an unmarried individual who actively avoided romantic relationships and was geographically distanced from my family.

It was not my intention to encounter my life partner in that particular setting. He had intentions of attending the Christian fellowship gathering at which I was present.

Jerry, however, had an expectation of encountering a female acquaintance. Consequently, he initiated a courtship with a different individual participating in the dance class prior to developing a deep understanding of her. They only went on a few occasions, and he did not experience profound emotional distress when she ceased to reply to his electronic communications and phone calls. However, had he exhibited greater perseverance, he could have spared himself some anguish.

When discussing engagement within the local community, my intention is not to do so with the ulterior motive of seeking a romantic partner. I imply that you should engage in such actions while considering the objective of acquainting yourself with various individuals within a collective setting.

I became cognizant of the possibility that I may have discovered my soul mate within the dance class upon witnessing a dance partner display a genuine attraction towards me during an evening performance. While he possessed both attractiveness and financial stability, my intuition suggested that he was not the suitable companion for me, prompting me to employ tactful avoidance.

Shortly thereafter, Jerry and I commenced dancing more frequently, and before long, he inquired about the possibility of us finding a suitable location to rehearse our acquired skills.

Do you comprehend the rationale behind my affirmative response? Apart from his attractiveness, it is noteworthy that he only approached me after we had ample opportunities to acquaint ourselves and I had developed a reliable intuition about his character.

In the preceding decade, I had been propositioned by a number of individuals. The majority of individuals appeared amicable, while a select few purportedly embraced spiritual convictions aligned with my own. Additionally, I discerned a preference for a couple of individuals based on their physical appeal.

Consequently, what was the reason for me declining their offer? In addition to the period in which I harbored negative feelings towards men, I found it noteworthy that they all approached me directly without prior acquaintance. I gleaned an invaluable experience during my youth, realizing the importance of not acquiescing to someone's invitation merely out of a lack of alternative engagements. After experiencing past disappointments, I became resolute in my determination to evade any similar instances of distress.

Enrolling in a dance class presents an excellent opportunity to familiarize oneself with a diverse array of gentlemen. However, there exist additional venues of similar nature.

The Process Of Identifying An Ideal Life Partner

Have you made the decisive choice to embark on a quest for your compatible life partner? Or you just want someone special in your life and only believe in the concept of dating? For every individual in this world, there invariably exists a potential individual who may manifest as their unique or exemplary romantic counterpart. It is imperative for you to comprehend that achieving an ideal partnership necessitates adhering to a set of prescribed measures.

Initially, it is necessary to establish your preferences in a potential partner. When seeking a partner, it is advisable to conduct a thorough self-assessment, evaluating both your strengths and weaknesses. This will assist you in selecting an exceptional partner. Numerous individuals possess a flawed perception that establishing a connection with another individual will augment the quality of their existence, fostering joy and thereby alleviating the emptiness in their routine activities. This assertion is clearly unfounded. Occasionally, an erroneous choice can engender a multitude of complications in one's life. It is of utmost importance that you select a suitable option for your needs. Prior to proceeding with your quest, it is imperative that you enhance and enhance the quality of your current lifestyle. Make an effort to develop constructive hobbies and habits, alter your lifestyle, and adopt a optimistic outlook on life. This can indeed have a positive impact on your relationship with your partner.

It is crucial to exhibit a high level of empathy and ensure explicit communication regarding your expectations from your significant other. Do you place significant emphasis on a partner's exceptional physical attractiveness? Are you, perchance, in search of an individual who possesses comparable idealistic tendencies? These criteria hold significant importance as they serve as the foundation of every subsequent relationship.

In contemporary society, the phenomenon of globalization has significantly constrained individuals' opportunities to engage in personal relationships. They lack the capability to select a suitable companion for themselves and are becoming progressively reliant on online dating platforms. Contemporary websites provide diverse services catering to individuals seeking guidance in selecting a suitable life partner. Consequently, numerous individuals are registering on online platforms to establish a balance between their professional commitments and personal endeavors.

It is important to comprehend that despite your utmost efforts, attaining a partner who exhibits flawlessness in every aspect may prove elusive. Indeed, it is an undeniable fact that nobody can attain perfection in every aspect. Interpersonal connections necessitate the cultivation of a constructive outlook and the capacity to embrace one's partner, flaws and all.

When commencing your quest for an ideal companion, initiate by frequenting social establishments frequented by a sizable congregation of individuals. Initiate the conversation by engaging in polite conversation regarding your leisurely activities, personal interests, and related topics.

Additionally, you may inform your family and friends of your current single status and express your openness to meeting potential partners. It is possible that one may be surprised by the effectiveness of such strategies on numerous occasions. You may have the opportunity to be introduced to an individual who could potentially be an ideal match for you.

Guide 3

What is the recommended duration for courtship before entering into a matrimonial union?

"Fundamentally, the act of engaging in a romantic relationship is akin to embarking upon the ascent of a volcano, with an inherent level of uncertainty as to the moment it may violently erupt, discharging searing molten materials that can cause great harm and inflict burns upon one's person." – Robin Bielman

Currently, there is a trend in which couples are opting to marry at a later stage in life compared to the previous generation. According to data obtained from the U.S. Census Bureau, the mean age of men at their initial marriage in 1970 was recorded as 23.2, whereas women generally entered into their first marriage at an average age of 20.8.

Presently, the mean ages stand at 29.8 and 28, correspondingly—exhibiting a noteworthy augmentation of more than ten years over the preceding half-century. 1. It is apparent that individuals are entering matrimony at an advanced age, however, were you aware that it has become increasingly customary for couples to engage in a prolonged period of dating and cohabitation prior to marriage?

During the women's liberation movement of the 1960s and '70s, there was a shift in the traditional view of marriage, transitioning from a focus on co-dependency and obligations to one centered around love and personal gratification. As a result, couples began to delay marriage and dedicate more time to nurturing their relationships while simultaneously pursuing their individual goals.

The majority of couples typically engage in courtship for a duration of two or more years prior to making a commitment to marry, displaying a common trend of dating ranging from two to five years. Upon the proposal, the customary duration of engagement typically ranges from 12 to 18 months.

The typical duration of a romantic partnership prior to entering into matrimony.

Although responses may vary, available data indicates that the typical timeframe for a relationship prior to marriage spans from two to five years. Merely because couples are deferring marriage does not imply that they are not establishing a shared existence. It has become increasingly common for couples to cohabit prior to their marriage, and societal norms have correspondingly evolved to embrace this trend.

Hendrix further asserts that the majority of couples he witnesses cohabitate as a precursor to entering into matrimony. According to the Pew Research Center's 2019 study, a significant number of couples choose to live together long-term, considering themselves in a marital relationship despite not being legally married. These couples may only choose to get married if they decide to have children, as the study found that two-thirds of individuals who cohabitated with their spouse before marriage viewed their cohabitation as a progression toward marriage.

Additionally, nearly fifty percent of the individuals surveyed expressed the belief that couples who reside together prior to marriage are more likely to experience a successful marital union compared to those who do not. Furthermore, a significant majority of 69% considered cohabitation to be morally acceptable, even in cases where the involved parties have no intention of entering into matrimony. The study further demonstrated that within the demographic of individuals aged 18 to 44, a significant majority of 59% had shared a residence with a partner to whom they were not legally married, at least once in their lifetime.

When posed with the question of whether it is advisable for couples to cohabit prior to getting married, Hendrix responds, "It is a matter of personal choice." If their relationship has mainly encompassed long-distance dating and they are considering marriage, then I strongly recommend that they allocate a period of time to cohabitate, in order to assess their compatibility and dynamics in the context of daily life together. What is the subject of their disagreement? Is it possible for them to reconcile after engaging in a conflict? Additionally, she holds the belief that if a couple is betrothed and only one partner exhibits strong resolve to marry in the near future, it is imperative for both parties to align their intentions regarding the wedding before making arrangements to

Select A Website, Establish Your Profile, And Determine Your Specific Preferences.

Discover an Optimal Online Dating Platform

Prior to beginning, it would be beneficial for you to conduct preliminary research. Commence the search for a reputable dating platform to explore. When embarking upon your search, it would be beneficial to establish certain fundamental criteria to employ in your assessment, such as verifying the absence of charges and evaluating high ratings, as exemplified. Establish the desired characteristics that you wish for it to possess, and subsequently conduct thorough research until you discover a suitable one. If one is in the nascent stages of seeking romantic connections, it is of utmost significance to seek out complimentary online dating platforms, particularly in the event that one has not yet reached a point of financial commitment in this pursuit. You should additionally ponder upon the type of association you desire, be it one of friendship or a platform catering to individuals seeking matrimonial partners.

Knowing What You Want

Prior to embarking on the creation of your personal profile, it is imperative to have a clear understanding of the specific criteria you seek in a potential partner. Are you seeking a committed and long-term relationship? Or perhaps you are interested in pursuing an arrangement akin to casual dating? It is imperative to address these inquiries initially in order to ascertain your desires prior to proceeding with the creation of your profile.

Certain women sometimes overlook the crucial aspect of possessing a clear understanding of their relationship requirements prior to creating a dating profile, consequently leading to challenges in establishing meaningful connections within the realm of online dating. The profiles of individuals who exhibited uncertainty about their preferences or intentions regarding relationships, or those who realized they lacked a clear understanding of their desires, might be classified as indecisive individuals. It is imperative not only to possess clarity regarding your relationship goals but also a profound understanding of the qualities you desire in a potential partner.

One valuable suggestion is to compile a catalogue of desirable qualities that you seek in a male individual, and subsequently, as you engage in conversations with potential candidates, ensure that said list remains at the forefront of your thoughts. It is essential to ensure that the individual you choose is genuinely someone of interest to you, thereby preventing you from becoming solely preoccupied with a man's physical qualities. There have been instances in which women engaged in conversations with men based solely on their physical appearance, investing time in dating these men despite their lack of the desired qualities.

Know Yourself!

After selecting a dating website and determining your criteria in a potential partner, you can initiate the process of creating your personal profile. The realm of online dating presents numerous potential opportunities and has the capacity to facilitate your acquaintance with individuals whom you would not have encountered otherwise. Nevertheless, prior to embarking on any exploration, it is imperative that due consideration be given to a key aspect: self-awareness. Make an effort to introspect on your preferences and aversions, your areas of interest and leisure activities, your personal principles and idiosyncrasies. Being cognizant of your identity and consistently bearing that knowledge in your thoughts will guarantee that you successfully ascertain your specific pursuits and establish a mutually desired connection with a gentleman who seeks an individual resembling yourself. Many women often struggle with the pressure to transform themselves in order to maintain the attention of an attractive man. However, in reality, you would simply be squandering valuable time by failing to be truthful with one another. Please bear in mind that individuals are actively seeking someone who meets their specific criteria. Therefore, it is of utmost importance to maintain authenticity in every conversation.

Create Your Profile!

At long last! Upon completing your extensive research, meticulous compilation of data, and thorough reflection, you have reached the pivotal moment of creating your very own online dating profile! Equipped with a comprehensive understanding of your identity and a clear vision of your preferences, you possess all the requisite information to successfully craft your profile. Please bear these lessons in mind during the process of creating your profile and when completing essential information. In order to finalize your profile, it is necessary to first complete a series of subsidiary steps.

Chapter 5: A Guide to Practicing Proactivity

Congratulations! By successfully establishing your profile, you have demonstrated proactive measures towards discovering a meaningful romantic connection. You are advised not to cease at this moment. A common error that I have frequently observed (and have personally experienced) is the tendency for individuals to create a profile and subsequently allow it to remain dormant. There are several factors that contribute to this occurrence, encompassing absentmindedness, anxiety, or the assumption that others will seek your assistance at this moment.

A simple method to mitigate forgetfulness would be to download and install the application affiliated with the respective dating platform on your mobile device. This feature promotes enhanced convenience by allowing users to readily access the platform at their convenience while providing the option to receive prompt notifications for likes and messages.

Regarding the anxiety, perceive your dating site encounter in the same manner as you would any unfamiliar situation: adopt the perspective (even if not entirely accurate) that everyone else shares the same level of nervousness as you. Dating platforms also enable individuals to express interest in others, even if they experience inhibitions in directly initiating conversation by sending a message. Frequently, these websites incorporate functionality referred to as "flirt" buttons (also identified as "like" or "favorite" buttons, as terminology may vary), allowing users to express their interest by simply clicking on the designated button. The individual shall be notified of your appreciation and may subsequently initiate a discussion with you. Additionally, these buttons can function as a means of bookmarking profiles that capture your interest. This way, should you desire to send them a message at a later time, locating them again will be convenient. Dating websites additionally facilitate the process of discerning mutual attraction. Frequently, in cases of mutual attraction, you will receive notification regarding your compatibility. Exercise caution, for it is common for individuals to express admiration solely on the basis of physical appeal.

The utilization of the "flirt" button embodies a somewhat passive approach, prompting me to propose conducting thorough research instead. I am implying that it would be beneficial for you to thoroughly examine their profile.

You may discover a substantial overlap in interests, making the process of initiating a conversation much more straightforward than anticipated. It is remarkable how finding a shared interest can instill a sense of comfort when commencing a conversation. If you discover that this is indeed the situation, refrain from hastily expressing exuberance by simply writing "Hi!" It is essential to demonstrate that you have invested time in reading their profile by including an intriguing aspect from it. The initial message you send serves as the foundation of your first impression. Convey your genuine interest to them. In the event that you choose to divulge your favorite film, it may be deemed endearing and clever to cite a favored line from said film. Alternatively, if you both share an interest in hiking, it may be beneficial to discuss some preferred trails.

It is entirely acceptable to compose a single sentence, yet do not hesitate to articulate your thoughts through several paragraphs if you deem it necessary. Exercise rational thinking, strive to captivate their interest, evoke affection, and incorporate humor; refrain from divulging your complete personal history, including your ambitions, aspirations, and anxieties, within the initial communication. While it can be quite gratifying to receive a lengthy message, messages of such nature can sometimes evoke a disconcerting impression and discourage recipients. The principle to adhere to is that one should refrain from engaging in online behavior that they would not exhibit in face-to-face interactions. This particular mistake ought not to require explicit mention, yet regrettably it does: It is strictly advised to refrain from initiating a message with a greeting such as "hey sexy," particularly when seeking a meaningful romantic connection. It lacks propriety and regard, and conveys misleading messages.

However, if you are initiating a polite and well-considered dialogue, do not hesitate to initiate the first exchange. It is highly appreciated when individuals are informed that they have captured someone's interest. In the event that the individual fails to respond, endeavor not to allow it to significantly impact you. Please proceed to review the remaining high-matching individuals on the list and engage in conversation with each of them as well. Rest assured, an individual will indeed initiate a discourse.

After initiating a conversation, it is advisable to continue and not abandon it at that point. Persist with the current connection, whilst simultaneously engaging in conversations with other potential candidates, in order to guarantee that you ultimately pursue a relationship with the most suitable individual.

Chapter One

How does one ascertain their soul mate connection? To begin with, it is imperative that you establish a clear understanding of your desired attributes in a life partner. In the event that you possess unwavering certainty regarding your ideal soul mate and perceive no necessity for contemplation, it is important to bear in mind that counterfeit gold bears a striking resemblance to genuine gold.

Create a comprehensive inventory enumerating the desirable attributes you seek in an ideal life partner, ensuring to document it meticulously for future reference and potential amendments. If the complexity of this exercise proves challenging or if you are uncertain about how to initiate it, commence by compiling a roster of the attributes that you do not desire in a prospective life partner. Based on this analysis, one can infer the desirable traits in a potential partner and proceed to document them.

Within this very exercise, picture the type of partnership that you share with your significant other. Please ensure that your responses are grounded in reality, as your ultimate goal is to find a genuine soul mate.

How do you and your significant other manage disagreements, ranging from minor differences to more intense arguments?

What is your preferred method for addressing and expressing your dissatisfaction with their behavior that has caused you distress?

How would you describe your emotional state upon encountering them following a day's work or a period of absence?

What are your sentiments when you partake in their company (in a relaxed setting within the residence or during outings in public)?

Conflicts are inherent components of robust relationships, and their resolution serves as an indicator of the relationship's level of maturity. The primary emphasis of this written exercise lies in the matter of security pertaining to transparent communication, truthfulness, aspiration, assurance, and ease. This is in addition to the attributes that you have previously documented as your criteria for an ideal life partner.

Meet People

The disintegration of communities has resulted in individuals experiencing a sense of seclusion. A significant number of individuals amongst us are unfamiliar with the identities of our neighbors and exhibit a lack of initiative to engage in social interactions. We all reside within the confines of our individual domains, preoccupied with our own affairs. There exist individuals who encounter challenges in establishing communication, leading to a profound sense of isolation. Individuals were not inherently intended for solitary existence, as social isolation fosters adverse effects on mental wellbeing.

There exist institutions dedicated to facilitating social interactions, for instance, places of worship such as churches. Seek out social organizations to engage in social interactions. There is a wide array of social groups featured on Facebook. You have the opportunity to participate in specialized interest groups, such as those centered around activities like hiking, yoga, games, painting, and similar pursuits. To initiate the process, navigate to the search bar on the Facebook.com homepage and manually input an activity that aligns with your interests, alongside specifying your city of residence. In order to connect with others, it is imperative to demonstrate creativity. It is not advisable to seek for a life partner in a bar or club, unless one desires to perpetuate that particular lifestyle. It would be unrealistic to anticipate that an individual, met at a drinking establishment, would completely abstain from consuming alcoholic beverages thereafter. You cannot change people. It would be advisable to seek a partner who shares compatible interests with you. Should you desire an individual with a genuine passion for culinary arts, consider enrolling in a cooking course. If your preference is for individuals with athletic prowess, consider becoming a member of a community sports team. To ensure compatibility with an individual who regularly attends religious services, it is imperative that you embody the same commitment and practice. Identify your interests and seek out environments where you can engage with like-minded individuals. Participate in a literary society, enroll in a community educational program, or become a member of a fitness facility, among other options. Gatherings such as Comic-Con can provide exceptional opportunities for individuals to connect with others. Partake in endeavors that bring you pleasure in order to encounter individuals who possess similar interests. It is possible for you to discover a partner via a shared acquaintance. Your acquaintances possess a deep understanding of your character and may have connections with individuals who could prove to be an ideal match for you. If one remains confined to their residence continuously, the prospect of establishing new acquaintances and social connections becomes notably improbable. It is highly unlikely that your soulmate will appear at your doorstep unannounced.

A significant majority of individuals establish relationships of friendship within the workplace, often failing to appreciate this fact. However, certain individuals are confined to their residences or are unable to engage in social interactions outside of working hours due to the absence of childcare options, among other circumstances. Enhancing the quality of individuals' lives through fostering social connections is of utmost significance. For instance, the implementation of a child-minding service operated by single parents would yield mutual advantages for all parties involved. Participating in an evening class and venturing outside the confines of one's home could prove to be a significant catalyst, fostering personal growth and unlocking a plethora of additional prospects.

Individuals who have been engaged in a committed, long-term relationship often encounter significant challenges when transitioning to the process of meeting new individuals. Their level of self-assurance might be currently at an unprecedented nadir. Dating agencies are flourishing and offer particular convenience for individuals who may have reservations about venturing into bars or clubs unaccompanied. It presents a more secure means of acquainting oneself with others.

Familiarize oneself with diverse individuals. Give them a chance. An individual whom you might initially lack attraction towards could potentially be the person who becomes the love of your life. Individuals who possess an appealing disposition and engender a delightful company tend to elicit increased levels of attraction in you. Outer looks fade. An individual may possess outer beauty, yet harbour inner qualities of great malevolence. It is not to be implied that all individuals possessing beauty are of an unpleasant nature. An individual lacking physical appeal can also possess unpleasant characteristics. Do not solely rely on appearance as the foundation of your judgment. The individual residing within that physical form is what holds significance. Seek out an individual who brings you joy and contentment.

Engaging in communal activities such as sporting endeavors constitutes an alternate approach. Developing friendships through participating in sports such as tennis or volleyball offers the advantage of shared interests and the added benefit of engaging in physical activity. Engaging in solitary activities such as watching television or playing computer games within the confines of one's home is acceptable, but it is not conducive to leading a fulfilling and purposeful existence. Not interacting with people becomes a habit. Gaming possesses the potential for sociability through engaging in online multiplayer experiences or partaking in cooperative play within the confines of one's residence. On occasion, we tend to replace our actual lived experiences with the lives of television personalities. Therefore, take the initiative to engage in the matter. Switch off the television and re-engage with the external environment. Regardless of whether you engage in voluntary activities or engage in leisure activities, you will be effectively conveying the notion of interpersonal interaction. You may potentially embark on an adventure of your own!

Get Away From Me!

Recall the occasion during your high school years when you entered the lunchroom and observed the distinct social groups congregating in segregated sections? There existed a distinctive group of individuals comprising the popular students, the athletes, the academically inclined, the individuals associated with substance use, the non-conformists, the individuals involved in theater and music, those who preferred solitude, the average students, and the remaining individuals. The section to which you migrated was a reflection of your personal determination regarding your rightful place.

Entering a room as a mature individual does not differ greatly from one's experience in high school. You conduct a comprehensive analysis of the individuals, assessing your compatibility with each group, and subsequently determine the most suitable environment for your integration. You stick with your crew and don't associate with "different" types. This is also applicable within the context of romantic relationships. One would refrain from initiating conversation with an individual who does not appear to meet their personal preferences, and if the said person were to initiate conversation instead, one would kindly acknowledge their presence with a smile and gracefully depart.

I propose that you provide an opportunity to every individual. It is possible that you may pleasantly discover an affectionate connection with an individual whom you would typically overlook. Appearances can be deceiving. Should one resort to assessments solely founded on appearances and hastily conclude that an individual does not align with their preferences prior to acquainting themselves with said individual, there is a distinct potential for the regrettable oversight of an exceptional individua

The meeting of a young lady residing nearby and a gentleman associated with punk rock culture

During a summer while in the employ of a talent agent, I attended a production at an off-off-Broadway theater in New York City. I received a complimentary ticket to an unfamiliar theatrical production, and as such, I made the decision to attend and experience it firsthand. Due to the sparsity of attendees, I selected a seat positioned along the aisle towards the rear of the theater, anticipating the possibility of promptly departing, as necessary. Typically, I opt for a seat situated at the forefront to closely observe the actors' facial expressions during theatrical performances; however, I deemed such a seating arrangement inappropriate on this occasion.

I noticed Ron instantly. He sported vibrant blue hair with a styled texture, adorned numerous piercings and tattoos that adorned his physique, and donned various chains that draped around his neck and waist. We established visual connection, after which I diverted my gaze. I must acknowledge that I made a premature assessment of him based solely on initial impressions. I perceived him approach with assurance in my periphery, and upon reaching my vicinity, he paused by my seating area and politely inquired if he could occupy the same space as me. As a newcomer to the city without any acquaintances, I timidly consented.

I had not anticipated the caliber of his character, but he ultimately proved to be an exceptional individual. He was in attendance to offer his support to his intimate acquaintance who was participating in the theatrical production. I was grateful for his audacious decision for numerous reasons. Initially, the performance failed to captivate my attention, and he persistently whispered trivial remarks in my vicinity. Additionally, he extended an invitation for me to join the cast for beverages following the event. I felt like a real New Yorker having drinks out at a bar! It was a weeknight, and I was shocked at how crowded the city was. Despite having been raised in large urban centers, I had never encountered a genuine nocturnal milieu akin to that of New York City until that particular evening.

Our romantic involvement persisted throughout the summer, until the point in time when I relocated. Any individual who encountered us while walking down the street likely perceived us as being utterly mismatched. I exuded an aura reminiscent of the archetype of the friendly, unassuming neighbor, possessing a naturally sweet and innocent demeanor. He appeared to resemble a member of a punk rock ensemble or heavy metal group. Given his appearance, I anticipated him to exhibit characteristics commonly associated with substance abusers; however, he demonstrated no inclination towards smoking or drug consumption. He displayed exceptional kindness and impeccable manners, earning my profound admiration and fostering a strong affinity towards him.

We formed a connection based on our shared passion for theater, and he graciously introduced me to the finest establishments in the city of New York. On a certain occasion, I inquired of him as to why he had approached me on that particular evening at the theater. His response was that it appeared that I was in need of companionship. That decision resulted in an exceptional outcome. I experienced the most fulfilling summer of my early adult years, during which I formed a genuine bond with an individual whom I would not typically regard as a potential partner.

Concluding my observation: It is important to refrain from making assumptions regarding others. Ron appeared to possess qualities that were entirely opposite to my own, and I had consistently refrained from engaging with individuals of his physical presentation in previous circumstances.

Fortunately, we possessed analogous dispositions and established a profound rapport on numerous fronts. Had I chosen to reject his invitation to accompany me at the theater, I would have missed out on the opportunity to partake in a remarkable summer romance with an exceptional gentleman.

Would it be permissible for me to utilize the restroom?

Being unfamiliar with Chicago, I received a call from my cousin, brimming with enthusiasm, informing me that he had an acquaintance he wished to introduce me to. I was open to the idea of acquainting myself with a new individual, particularly one who had been recommended by my cousin. His given name was Andrew, and he was an accomplished individual in the field of stockbroking. He appeared exceptionally attractive in the photograph, and it was conveyed to me that we shared parallel backgrounds.

Upon meeting Andrew in person several days later, it became apparent that he perfectly matched my preferences. I was immediately drawn to him, and I was eager to acquire comprehensive knowledge about his essence. We dined at an upscale restaurant for dinner, and afterwards, he graciously extended an invitation for me to visit his condominium to enjoy a movie together. Under normal circumstances, I would never consent to visiting the residence of an unfamiliar individual for our initial encounter. Nevertheless, considering the fact that my cousin maintained a friendship with Andrew and possessed knowledge of his place of residence, I believed it to be a secure situation.

His condo was breathtaking. Meticulously crafted with stunning furnishings, and situated in a high-end edifice. We took seats on his opulent couch and engaged in conversation for a period of time. In the midst of an uncomfortable silence during our conversation, he nonchalantly extended his hand towards the remote control, utterly intent on locating a suitable program to view. He briefly skimmed through the channels and subsequently paused upon noticing that the movie Lolita was on the verge of commencing. With great enthusiasm, he expressed his preference for the movie, which led me to consent to watching it. I was previously unaware of its existence, but subsequently, I uncovered that the movie centered around a pedophile. An unconventional selection for a preferred film, wouldn't you agree? The plot of Lolita was intriguing, thereby providing me with a satisfactory level of entertainment.

Upon the conclusion of the film, I requested permission to avail myself of the lavatory facilities, and it was at this juncture that events took an unusual and unexpected course. Possibly, he may have been in an animated state following the observation of the intimate interactions involving an adult male and a fourteen-year-old female. Alternatively, one could surmise that the act of viewing his preferred film elicited his inherent malevolence. Regardless of the circumstances, I had not anticipated that a routine trip to the bathroom would transform into a remarkable encounter. Here's what happened:

May I have permission to utilize your restroom?

Andrew: "Sure. It's right through there."

He indicated to a door situated across the living room, prompting me to commence moving toward it.

Andrew abruptly exclaimed, "Hold on!" as he swiftly rose to his feet and materialized directly in front of me. Rather than urinating on me, would you be willing to do so in a different manner? I have harbored a long-standing desire for someone to urinate on me."

Me: I was astounded, and I remained immobile in that moment.

Andrew: "Kindly reconsider. It will be an extraordinary experience." There is nobody observing or critiquing your actions."

Me: "Uhhhh…"

Andrew: Imploringly, "Please, join us." I experience a strong sense of ease and liberation in your presence."

Me: The initial surprise dissipated, and my cognition swiftly became inundated with a myriad of thoughts. 1. What is the matter with this eccentric individual? 2. Would it be advisable for me to proceed and conclude the task promptly? 3. I am in dire need of using the restroom. 4. May I swiftly retrieve my handbag and evacuate this premises? 5. Perhaps I will ultimately derive pleasure from the experience. 6. Could he potentially request a degrading or humiliating act from me in the future? 7. I am in need of relieving my bladder urgently. 8. Will he have a favorable reaction to the flavor if it comes into contact with his oral cavity? 9. Is he regarding this as a form of prelude? 10. I am required to make a decision.

Andrew: He perceived my lack of decisiveness and inferred that as acquiescence to urinate on him. He reclined upon the carpeted surface directly adjacent to my presence, and proceeded to elevate his shirt.

Me: As an innocent and inexperienced woman, I figured I'd give it a try. I pondered the possibility, wondering if this inclination might develop into a personal preference of mine. I positioned myself above him, straddling his trunk while gradually removing my garments. I assumed a crouched posture and gazed unwaveringly into his voracious gaze. At that juncture, my bladder had reached an extreme state of distension, verging on the point of rupture, yet regrettably, I found myself incapable of voiding even a single droplet of urine. After a brief pause, I nodded in negation and stated with regret, "I apologize, but it is unlikely to occur." Subsequently, I readjusted my clothing, proceeded towards the restroom, and relieved myself by expelling the contents into the toilet.

Upon my return to the living room, I discovered him seated on the sofa, exhibiting an air of defeat. It was mutually understood that there was no further discourse or action to pursue. I expressed my gratitude for the dinner and took my leave. We never spoke again. Looking back on that night, I will say that I never felt scared or unsafe. Fortunately, he exhibited exemplary manners. Despite his request for me to urinate on him, he refrained from exerting force, raising his voice, or resorting to any form of violence. He respectfully made a request, and despite my best efforts, I was unable to fulfill it. It is highly preposterous that he made a request for me to urinate on him, an act which I categorize as of a sexual nature, despite the fact that throughout the entire evening, we neither embraced nor exchanged any form of physical intimacy that could be construed as sexual.

My conclusion: An individual possessing an attractive residential property, supportive social network, and prosperous professional trajectory might exhibit unconventional or erratic behavior. Despite the arrangement made by your acquaintance or family member, they lack insight into his true demeanor when you find yourself in his company without any external influences. My cousin believed that Andrew would be the most suitable partner for me. Perhaps his qualifications appeared suitable on paper; however, there are additional aspects to consider in a relationship beyond mere criteria.

Summary

Do not prematurely judge an individual's character or disposition solely on the basis of their physical appearance or personal background. It is imperative to afford all individuals an equitable opportunity. It is possible that you may develop an attraction towards an individual who does not align with your typical preferences, or you may come to realize that aligning with certain desirable characteristics on paper does not necessarily indicate compatibility in reality. Engaging in collaborative exploration can be an enjoyable and beneficial undertaking, but it is advisable to reserve such experiences for the context of a committed partnership.

Step 1. Attain Clarity Regarding Your Desires

Devote some time in contemplation and reflect upon the qualities that you envision in your ideal partner.

Please provide information regarding their character traits.

Are they funny?

Are the really smart?

Are they ambitious? This location is not conducive to exhibiting gold digging tendencies and harboring desires for considerable wealth. Material wealth does not inherently contribute to an individual's overall sense of happiness or well-being. Certain individuals may encounter the need to begin anew in life, and it is imperative to recognize that their personal worth should not be determined by the balance in their bank account. Lacking ambitious aspirations, one may encounter significant obstacles in attaining elevated positions.

What are the ethical principles and values that they uphold? (I refrained from examining this matter together with my former spouse, resulting in significant discord between us.)

Do they possess an affinity for children, do they have offspring, or do they abstain from parenting?

It is imperative that if one has children, they possess a significant fondness for children. If one has no desire or inability to have children, it is important to seek a partner who shares the same viewpoint or already has children in their life. This situation carries significant implications that may lead to profound unhappiness for one party within the couple, particularly in cases where one desires children while the other does not. Avoid this mistake.)

If you are in possession of progeny or planning to procreate, what convictions do they hold regarding the art of child-rearing? This incident marked another significant confrontation between my former spouse and myself. This particular matter holds significant importance.

Do they possess a propensity for athleticism or engage in a physically active lifestyle?

Are they fond of traveling?

Do they possess gainful employment?

Are they a felon? I made several mistakes in this regard as well. Dang bad boys!)

Do they make efforts towards self-improvement?

Are they affectionate? In the event that one individual possesses a predisposition for affection while their partner does not, or conversely, it can give rise to difficulties.

What is their demeanor in the presence of others? Do they have a social nature or do they prefer to remain private?

What is the manner in which they attend to your needs?

Do they have manners?

What is the manner in which they engage with and care for your family?

Do they exhibit a sense of encouragement towards your aspirations?

Do they display acceptance towards your social interactions?

I could elaborate at length, but I strongly encourage you to allocate 10-15 minutes towards considering various aspects, characteristics, and qualities. What qualities would your ideal partner possess? Don't hold back. If one were to craft a mystical elixir with the intention of summoning an ideal companion, utmost specificity would be advisable.

Proceed to review your list once more and indicate with a circle those items that are categorized as essential requirements and those that are considered desirable but not essential.

Please proceed with completing the exercise located on the subsequent page.

Obtain the complimentary workbook at no cost by clicking the link provided.

Action Step 1. Establish Clarity Regarding Your Desires - How Would an Ideal Companion Mirror My Preferences?

Please address all the inquiries found on the preceding page and identify your essential priorities by enclosing them within circles.

Step 2. What attributes or qualities would you prefer your ideal partner not possess?

This holds great significance. Failing to account for the negative aspects and solely focusing on the positives can lead to undesired consequences reminiscent of opening a proverbial can of worms. Be specific here too. Allocate a 10-15 minute interval to conscientiously consider the aspects that you do not desire to have in your life. Here are a handful of options to commence your journey.

They should refrain from harboring feelings of jealousy.

They should refrain from exerting control.

I prefer to associate with individuals of integrity.

I prefer not to have someone who harbors an aversion towards children.

I have no desire for individuals who belittle others.

I prefer to associate with individuals who demonstrate a higher level of cleanliness and tidiness.

I have no desire for individuals who exhibit discriminatory tendencies.

I prefer not to associate with individuals who engage in continuous and exclusive indulgence in video gaming.

I prefer individuals who exhibit emotional stability and maintain composure in challenging situations.

I would prefer to engage with individuals who have established their own independent living arrangements. "(Except in the event that it is Matthew McConaughey.) LOL)

Again, this list can go on and on. Devote sufficient time to compile a comprehensive inventory, subsequently revisiting it to identify essential exclusions or conditions, as well as distinguishing them from mere preferences.

Please proceed to perform the exercise located on the subsequent page at this time. Access the complimentary workbook by clicking the link provided.

Action Step 2. What attributes or qualities do you prefer your ideal partner not to possess?

Please respond to all inquiries presented on the preceding page, ensuring to encircle any qualities or attributes that your ideal partner should not possess.

Step 3. Understand the Value You Bring to the Discussion

Kindly dedicate a moment to compile a comprehensive list enumerating the qualities, attributes, and contributions that you possess and can actively offer in a romantic partnership.

Please candidly evaluate and enumerate the favorable attributes you contribute to a relationship.

Please provide a summary of your previous endeavors or efforts in developing successful relationships.

What remarkable qualities do you possess?

Please elaborate on your aspirations and objectives.

What are the positive qualities or behaviors that you typically exhibit?

What are the thoughts that you internally express regarding the notion that if others were aware of this specific aspect of your persona, they would harbor affection and acceptance towards you?

Direct your attention solely towards the positive aspects at present and solely contemplate your accomplishments thus far. This does not align with the version of yourself that you aspire to be, rather, it reflects your current state and past experiences.

Do the exercise on the next page now. Please access the complimentary workbook by downloading it here.

Action Step 3. Recognize and leverage the value you bring to this context

Please allocate a moment to compile a comprehensive inventory of the assets and qualities you possess that contribute to a successful relationship.

Step 4. What unfavorable habits or characteristics do you possess?

What are the habits or characteristics that you possess or have possessed in the past, which have proven to be problematic?

Once again, it is imperative that you maintain absolute honesty with yourself. In order to reach your intended destination, it is imperative to establish one's current location. This location is not suited for engaging in self-criticism. I kindly request that you openly and explicitly acknowledge that these concerns are mine. We all have issues. I will enumerate a few items below to assist you.

I have jealousy issues.

I have a higher body mass index and suboptimal physical fitness.

I do not attend to my personal well-being.

I hold a strong distaste for my current occupation which greatly impacts various aspects of my personal life.

I allocate a greater portion of my time towards interacting with my friends as compared to the amount of time I spend with my partner.

I get mad easy.

I do not derive satisfaction from engaging in sexual activities.

I struggle with my sense of self-worth.

I am a slob.

I am lazy.

You grasp the concept. Allocate a brief period of 5-10 minutes to engage in introspection and sincerely reflect on your thoughts and feelings. Please proceed to review the list and identify and highlight major issues that are likely to adversely impact any relationship, distinguishing them from lesser concerns that may simply be bothersome. If these are not to your liking, you have the ability to rectify each and every one of them. In order to attain a commendable partner, it is imperative that we exert our utmost efforts towards self-improvement. It goes both ways. In the event of significant concerns arising without a solution readily available, I am capable of offering my assistance in resolving them. Please do not hesitate to contact me.

The Mechanics Behind the Operation of the Law of Attraction

Once one gains a comprehensive understanding of the Law of Attraction and accurately comprehends its functioning, it becomes possible to embark upon a journey of self-discovery, ascertain the ideal life partner, attain genuine happiness and abundance, and ultimately realize one's cherished aspirations.

In the realm of Quantum Physics, the Law of Attraction is delineated as the phenomenon through which bodies or particles display a propensity to congregate or unite, forming a cohesive mass that exhibits resistance against disintegration. Put simply, it asserts that similar actions are inclined to attract similar actions.

An action refers to a deed carried out, an undertaking executed, typically with the aim of achieving an objective. Various synonymous terms include labor, motion, undertaking, procedure, demonstration, and endeavor. Cogitation is an incessantly carried out process, the endeavor we engage in to the greatest extent.

Presented below are several assertions aimed at elucidating the mechanisms underlying the functioning of the Law of Attraction:

Similar actions tend to invoke similar reactions.

• Similar actions elicit similar responses.

- Similar frequencies naturally attract each other.
- Similar types of energy have a tendency to attract one another.
- The phenomenon of like energy being drawn to like energy is evident.
- Energy with similar characteristics tends to gravitate towards one another.
- Like energy is magnetically attracted to comparable forms of energy.
- The principle that similar energies attract each other is observed.
- Those of similar nature are naturally drawn to one another.
- Like thought attracts like thought.
- The association of similar beliefs attracts one another.
- The alignment of similar intentions creates magnetic attraction.

A proclivity for engaging in certain activities tends to bring about a propensity for similar activities.

- The act of generosity tends to elicit reciprocal acts of generosity.

Individuals often face difficulties in their endeavors to leverage the Law of Attraction for the purpose of accomplishing their aspirations due to a lack of comprehensive comprehension pertaining to the concept that similar actions attract similar outcomes. There exist a multitude of individuals who will assert that the Law of Attraction operates by manifesting what occupies your predominant thoughts or by aligning with your conviction to attain. According to the belief that "energy follows thought" and considering thought as an action, therefore...

1. By directing your mental energy towards your desires and visualizing them within your mind,

2. Can vividly visualize and experience oneself with or as it.

3. And will carry out this task diligently and unwaveringly until it has come to fruition.

4. You shall draw towards yourself or transform into that which you long for.

While there exists some truth in this assertion, it is important to acknowledge that the overlooked aspect of like action attracting like action is a significant factor contributing to the failure to attain desired outcomes in creative thought. Let me better explain. I have the ability to envision anything I desire through the power of my thoughts, and I can dedicate my complete attention to it. I can sincerely believe that it will come to fruition, but its manifestation in my reality is contingent upon my genuine emulation of it through my actions.

All of our endeavors constitute actions, encompassing thoughts, emotions, verbal expressions, and behavior—any endeavor that expends mental or physical energy. The aggregate of all these actions corresponds to the resultant outcome, namely, our production or contribution to the world. The energy frequency we emit through our actions and outputs influences our resonance or affinity, subsequently determining the type of energy or opportunities that we draw towards us.

We reap what we sow, in accordance with our actions. Actions of a similar nature tend to draw actions of a similar nature.

All things are in a state of vibration, adhering to the principles governing the Law of Vibration. Each individual possesses a distinct frequency, vibration, or resonance that is established by the cumulative impact of their actions. Our previous deeds shape our current state of affairs, while our ongoing actions determine our forthcoming circumstances. We exert effort and subsequently receive an equivalent outcome.

One must authentically embody the qualities or characteristics they desire or aspire to possess, and align themselves with its inherent frequency, resonance, or melody. It is imperative to bestow willingly that which you desire to receive. One's character, actions, and generosity determine the kind of qualities, opportunities, and relationships they attract, rather than merely longing for them. The law is impervious to deception! "Do not be led astray; one cannot deceive God, as whatever one sows, so shall they reap" (Galatians 6:7).

Actions are motivated by one's beliefs; our conduct is influenced by our underlying convictions. The alteration of one's reality is governed by belief, as it impels the individual and collective senses and behaviors. Hence, Christ informed those individuals who sought healing from him that their restored well-being was truly attributed to "their unwavering faith" or "their profound belief." Each and every one of our actions can be likened to seeds that bear fruit, multiplying in accordance with their own nature. These actions are derived from our fundamental beliefs regarding the distinction between truth and falsehood.

I am unequivocally convinced of the existence of the Natural and Universal Laws, as my certainty stems from meticulous observation and experimentation conducted within the confines of my own life. "Are you acquainted with the decrees of the celestial realm?" (Job 38:33) Do not dismiss the laws of energy God set in place, learn about them to increase your understanding.

The principle of cause and effect, commonly referred to as the Law of Attraction or Karma, elucidates the immutable perfection of divine justice endorsed by God. Think about it. If we consistently receive in proportion to what we give, what could be fairer?

I can envision no superior blessing bestowed upon us by our Divine Creator than the privilege of being guided by a law that epitomizes equity and benevolence. The fate of our safeguard or ruin, our recompense or chastisement, lies within our own agency and is predicated exclusively on the generosity we elect to bestow upon others of our volition.

This is the precise reason why the Golden Rule holds significant significance, as conveyed by Christ when he stated, "Therefore, in all circumstances, treat others as you would like them to treat you. For this principle encapsulates the entirety of the Law, encompassing all the Natural and Universal Laws, as well as the teachings of the Prophets." (Matthew 7:12)

Additionally, he states, "By the same token, one's judgment of others will ultimately determine the extent and manner in which they are judged, as the measure employed will be applied reciprocally" (Matthew 7:2). He emphatically stated that it will indeed occur, rather than positing the possibility of its occurrence.

The actions you take shall be reciprocated unto you. The actions you take will inevitably result in consequences being reciprocated. This constitutes the paramount teaching imparted by authentic prophets, and it represents the utmost significance that necessitates your acquisition and application in all facets of your existence.

One might argue that this assertion lacks veracity, as numerous facets of existence often appear arbitrary and unjust. As an illustration, consider the scenario wherein an individual becomes a victim of homicide without any discernible motive, particularly in instances where they themselves have not committed such an act against another.

The deity proclaimed, "Whosoever takes individuals into subjugation shall themselves find themselves captive; those who cause death by wielding a blade shall face the same fate." "Behold, the saints demonstrate both fortitude and unwavering devotion" (Revelation 13:10).

Reincarnation stands as my proposed resolution to this perplexing dilemma. One may hold the perspective that reincarnation lacks biblical or Christian backing, thereby raising doubts or disbelief in its validity. Nevertheless, it is the sole explanation that can account for numerous statements made by Jesus, including the aforementioned quotation.

Considering the nature of this text does not revolve around the topic of reincarnation, I would like to direct your attention to an alternative resource that does explore this subject. I suggest referring to the book titled "Why Jesus Taught Reincarnation" authored by Herbert Bruce Puryear, Ph.D., published by New Paradigm Press in 1992.

The principle of the Law of Attraction perpetually operates, exerting its sway over the learning experiences of our soul across multiple incarnations. It is highly advantageous to familiarize yourself with its governing activity as promptly as possible.

The Law of Attraction may also be referred to as the Law of Giving or the Law of Love. Love not only reciprocates the genuine choices you make to extend kindness to others, but it also grants you precisely the necessary provisions at each juncture to progress towards completeness.

In order to discern the perpetual healing opportunities bestowed by the Law of Attraction, which is synonymous with the Law of Love and the epitome of impartial Blind Justice, one must possess perceptive faculties of the spirit, characterized by clear-sightedness and acute auditory acuity.

If you desire to modify your vibration or frequency and consequently shape what you are drawing towards you (or absorbing), it is vital that you display a readiness to adapt the nature of your expressions or outputs. It is crucial to remember that all entities possess a vibrational nature, wherein vibration manifests as kinetic activity, and akin to this concept, similar activities tend to be drawn towards one another.

Your assessments of individuals serve as mirrors that reflect your own image and resonate with your own similarity. This is intended to facilitate your ability to adapt your behavior, refine your resonance, and align it with the harmonious melody of love. Love is the sole force capable of assuaging the profound emptiness within oneself. The objective is to achieve a state of harmonious convergence with love, through embodying and manifesting love itself.

One's character is reflective of the judgments they make about others. The reflection they offer serves as a means by which you may identify and acknowledge the aspects of oneself that are present within. The reflection of what you draw towards yourself, be it a thought, individual, happening, or situation, is analogous. Through gazing into that mirror, one has the opportunity to behold their soul directly, provided they possess the audacity to unveil their spiritual sight and auditory perception.

Every introspection, whether it is perceived as an emotion or appraisal, presents an occasion to unveil one's authentic self at the core of their being, ascertain their purpose in existence, and identify the invaluable wisdom required to progress towards the subsequent phase on the journey that inevitably culminates in a sacred union with the benevolent embrace of Divine Love.

If the sentiments you hold toward individuals or circumstances deviate from a disposition of love, they serve as indicators highlighting the need for you to refine and amend your own comprehension.

The accuracy of your perception of reality, as well as the nature of your beliefs regarding yourself and others, can be determined by how they are reflected back to you. In this context, love serves as the assessing standard. Affection is the sole veracity. All that is devoid of love is fallacious, transient, and necessitates the elimination from our individual characters and spirits.

Modern Limits

Various manifestations of respect exist. An indicative indication suggesting that he is sincere and committed for the long haul emerges right from the early stages of dating, be it the initial encounter or the subsequent rendezvous. He will not be available for dating until he has determined his position with respect to you. He recognizes the scarcity of finding women of quality and is interested in assessing the merits you possess, as well as reciprocating by showcasing his own. During the second date, he will have likely determined if he wishes to proceed with the possibility of a romantic relationship and formulated an internal label for it. Many individuals in contemporary society, particularly when engaging in casual relationships, exhibit a lack of personal limits and readily disregard the consequences of their actions, prioritizing momentary pleasure without any hesitation. They possess an inclination to live each day without concern for the future. Regardless of the circumstances, if we develop affection for someone, we will not permit any obstacles to hinder the establishment of a flawless relationship. Indeed, we are willing to eliminate any factors that may lead to discordance or friction. We are willing to make significant sacrifices to demonstrate our unwavering dedication to the relationship, should anything cause you to reconsider.

Contemporary mobile devices now encapsulate and enable easy access to the entirety of our lives. Furthermore, they possess our confidential information. If you are capable of discreetly inspecting his phone at any given moment to satisfy your curiosity, without arousing any suspicion on his part, it indicates his genuine commitment to you, as he has no reason to conceal anything. He ought to instinctively reflect upon his actions that might have led to the formation of these unfavorable sentiments towards him, and earnestly consider measures to promptly rectify the situation. During such instances, it is expected that he conforms to your instructions, as he is aware of the necessity and desires you to have a clear perception of him. This demonstrates that he esteems you above his own ego.

It is imperative that you consistently evaluate our relationship until you have established a solid commitment with him, reflecting upon whether he genuinely appreciates and respects your worth. Or is his desire solely directed towards you?

Financial autonomy constitutes a significant aspect that necessitates your careful consideration. He is not necessarily required to have financial stability, but he should be willing to accept the responsibility of being capable of financially supporting you within the relationship. Inquire if it would be permissible to request a loan of £200 from him on a subsequent occasion, abstaining from doing so on the initial encounter to avoid any potential perception of opportunism. When the third meeting arises, inform him of an unforeseen situation of urgency necessitating the funds, offering assurance that repayment would be promptly made within a few months' time. If he executes the action promptly and without any reservations, it reflects his confidence and faith in you. If he is unable to lend you the money, it may give rise to a separate set of inquiries that you should consider. As an illustration, it is possible that he continues to reside in his parental residence. Should he engage in such behavior, it is highly probable that his actions are still being influenced by his mother. Perhaps he is seeking your support and assistance. You have assumed the role of his caregiver, however, he is receiving his entitlements from you. It would be deemed lacking value if he were unable to accomplish this straightforward task.

If you happen to be a single parent, and he also falls into that category. There is no greater displeasure than his amiable relationship with his former partner. There is a valid explanation for why she is no longer in a relationship with him, and there should be no doubt or inquiries regarding this matter. If he maintains an amicable relationship with his ex, it is likely that they engage in occasional intimate encounters, and it is possible that you are presently serving as a rebound until he reaches a definitive decision regarding this complex circumstance. The presence of children can occasionally lead to significant complexities; there is a chance that his former partner is expecting his offspring. Exercise patience with him as he may still be grappling with his emotions, unbeknownst to himself. It would be prudent to wait until the baby is born before making any decisions about continuing the relationship. At that time, both parties will have a clearer understanding of his level of commitment. In addition, there is no evident justification for his nocturnal absence with his children, when suddenly, his former partner appears. This serves as a significant indication to terminate the relationship.

Men possess an innate propensity for enigmatic emotional expressions. It has the potential to be authentic, yet simultaneously exhibit qualities of insincerity. As previously mentioned, if he allocates time for your company, it signifies his interest in pursuing a committed relationship. Conversely, if he fails to do so, it suggests that his intentions are solely focused on engaging in sexual activities. He might assert that he engages in perpetual labor to forge a more prosperous future for both himself and you. Engages with you solely for sexual encounters. It would be advisable to release him. He might offer an explanation for his emotional detachment, such as feeling unprepared for a committed relationship due to past infidelity in his previous relationship, yet displaying a willingness to engage in intimate encounters with you. He possesses a clear understanding of his expectations from you, constituting his unmistakable agenda.

Consistently exhibiting the willingness to share one's thoughts and emotions with you, even during moments of disagreement, demonstrates his unwavering support and presence in your life. Many men view this as an ideal pretext for infidelity, and subsequently absolve themselves of any responsibility by claiming an inability to effectively communicate their emotions. Sincere individuals who genuinely admire you will consistently refrain from escalating conflicts and ensuring that your emotional state remains unequivocal. In the event that you determine the need for a respite and abruptly depart, should you contact him, he will promptly extend his support to you. Various emotions can diverge and persist within his heart.

Distinguishing your desires and maintaining absolute conviction become effortless by recognizing your singular position. It can be quite challenging for an individual of the male gender to display vulnerability within a romantic partnership. Many women can confuse this with being needleless. Honorable men of integrity do not shy away from expressing their emotions towards you. He is aware that you bring added value to his life, and he is committed to reciprocating by enriching yours as well. Expressing one's genuine emotions does not denote a lack of strength. Being in a state of vulnerability does not equate to harboring feelings of insecurity. Upstanding gentlemen demonstrate diligent care, whether it be engaging in meaningful exchanges or tending to practical needs such as preparing a bath for one. Regardless, he is aware that women consistently receive attention from men, and he acknowledges that you belong to him and holds you in high regard.

From Friendship To Love

Getting to truly know an individual necessitates a considerable amount of time. The frequency of your communication with someone you have encountered on the Internet will determine the outcome. There exists a substantial disparity between cultivating a mere acquaintanceship and nurturing a bond wherein an intense allure is concurrently experienced towards said friend.

If you find yourself experiencing genuine attraction towards your cyberfriend, caution must be exercised, as it is plausible that your interest in them may not be reciprocated. Typically, this occurs when searching for an individual on the internet, which underscores the importance of proceeding with caution if one experiences a sense of excitement or anticipation upon receiving emails from their online acquaintance. Initially, it is imperative that you establish a sufficient level of familiarity with him. Engage in discussions pertaining to his interests, cultural aspects, music preferences, and sporting activities. By employing this approach, you will gain insight into your shared interests and foster a solid online friendship.

The concept of finding love through a computer remains challenging and is met with skepticism by many individuals who find it hard to believe. There are also individuals who are seeking love for the first time through online platforms, but they harbor uncertainty regarding the feasibility of a successful outcome. Individuals such as myself, who have undergone this particular encounter, possess a unique comprehension of how friendships can swiftly evolve into profound affection."

The foundation of love lies in the presence of a strong friendship, wherein one discovers an individual who genuinely embodies care and concern for their well-being. You and your online companion will ascertain the shared interests and similarities that exist between you. He elicits laughter from afar and consistently provides support during moments of low spirits, melancholy, or when experiencing a difficult day.

Upon completion of your subscription to the Online Dating Site, you will anticipate discovering that cherished partner whom you seek. You shall encounter not only one cybernaut, perchance a multitude, yet it shall be amongst them that one shall stand apart from the remainder. You have the potential to establish a strong friendship and potentially cultivate a mutual attraction, which may lead to the development of romantic sentiments. Engaging in conversation with him will elicit a sense of importance, not only for him but also for you. This pivotal moment signifies an elevated stage of friendship, signifying a shift beyond mere companionship.

Initially, Mark and I corresponded on a weekly basis, but subsequently, we increased the frequency to biweekly and ultimately progressed to daily exchanges. We developed a strong friendship, experiencing great contentment from maintaining regular communication and enjoying harmonious interactions. We were perpetually preoccupied with thoughts of one another, thereby transcending the physical distance and establishing a profound mental connection. Our bond grew to the extent that we no longer relied solely on computer screens for communication. I experienced a cherished sense of anticipation upon returning home or arriving at work, as I would often find a message from Mark, wherein he shared details of his daily existence and consistently displayed a keen interest in learning about my own.

The Chemistry

Undoubtedly, the presence of attraction through online means is a distinct possibility, which may manifest itself at any point in time once one discovers a genuine affinity towards their digital companion. His profile exhibited the very qualities that align with your desired attributes in a male individual, and as you engaged in correspondence with him, you have discerned a profound admiration for his character and discovered a notable convergence of common interests. Both parties have engaged in the exchange of pictures, thereby establishing a tangible attraction. Furthermore, a harmonious rapport has been established, reflected by an increase in communication frequency through email. The presence of chemistry between the individuals is apparent, leading to the emergence of novel emotional experiences with this cyber companion.

I vividly recall the profound sense of elation that enveloped me upon accessing my email and discovering a correspondence from my esteemed online acquaintance. These messages had an indelible impact, imbuing me with a profound sense of significance, and this sentiment would persist indefinitely. Initially, it may pose a challenge to fathom the notion that an individual residing far from your physical vicinity could genuinely integrate themselves into your life, imparting a sense of care and affection through remote communication devices. However, it is foreseeable that the prospect of cultivating an intimate connection online may soon manifest as a tangible actuality, allowing for the potential to engender romantic feelings towards an individual dwelling in a foreign nation.

When two individuals possess a deep affinity and captivating interest for one another, it signifies a significant connection and compatibility that renders them an ideal couple. It will become apparent if there is mutual attraction between you and your virtual companion, thereby transitioning your relationship beyond mere friendship.

It is imperative to ascertain one's own emotions with utmost certainty, as well as ensuring that one's Cyberfriend reciprocates the identical sentiments. There have been instances wherein the woman exhibits an interest in the cyberfriend, while he, on the other hand, shows no reciprocal interest and lacks any intention of advancing the relationship. He possesses qualities of amiability, politeness, and affability, but his attributes are limited to that extent. Consequently, the woman, who developed romantic feelings for him, eventually finds herself disillusioned. That is why it is important to know your cyberfriend well to be sure about his feelings and that he is actually romantically interested in you.

When receiving electronic communications from your online acquaintance, it is advised to not only peruse the contents, but also analyze the subtle cues he conveys through his written correspondence. If a man consistently bestows praise upon a woman, demonstrating genuine concern and affection, it indicates a distinct inclination towards her. However, it is important to note that individuals of the male gender possess diverse personalities and, consequently, may exhibit varying indicators. He may present himself as a reserved individual, displaying signs of interest towards you, yet struggling to overtly convey his true emotions. Ultimately, regardless of the circumstances, it will be necessary for you to determine whether there exists a mutual attraction between you and your cyber acquaintance. Even an individual with significant social hesitations will eventually find a means of expressing their interest, thereby initiating a potential romantic connection facilitated through the Internet.

Falling in Love Online

In what manner can one ascertain that they are developing affectionate feelings for their cyber companion? You frequently contemplate the thoughts revolving around the individual who consistently corresponds with you, questioning whether he reciprocates similar sentiments towards you. You and your cyberfriend engage in candid discussions, openly addressing any situation, including problems. Furthermore, both of you willingly exchange details about your daily lives, encompassing topics related to family and work. At some point, either you or he will have the opportunity to initiate a conversation regarding matters of love. It is possible that you might be curious as to why your cyberfriend currently lacks a partner, just as he may also hold the same curiosity towards you.

You both share a strong rapport and have already established a deep level of trust, making discussions about love an organic progression. This is the juncture where a friendship has the potential to transcend into a different realm if there is mutual attraction. The frequency of chat meetings and emails will increase progressively, as you will engage in telephone conversations and receive gifts via postal mail. Certain individuals will exert considerable effort to capture the interest of the woman they admire, employing gestures such as sending her floral arrangements and confectionery delicacies. A woman who receives a unique gift from her online acquaintance will undoubtedly experience a sense of exhilaration. However, I would recommend approaching the situation with caution, and it would be wise to begin by posing a few inquiries:

Do you experience a sense of unease or apprehension when engaging in online communication with your cyberfriend or when hearing their voice through a telephone call?

Do you frequently view his photographs?

Are you ruminating on his thoughts while engaging in activities such as listening to music or savoring a cup of coffee?

Upon accessing your email inbox, do you prioritize the opening of emails exclusively from your cyberfriend, deferring the opening of any other messages to a later time? If you have responded affirmatively to all of these inquiries, it is undeniable that you harbor deep affection for your online acquaintance.

On the occasion of Valentine's Day, Mark presented me with an extravagant arrangement of flowers for the very first time. He engaged the services of an international shipping company and instructed them to transport the items to the previous workplace I was affiliated with. It was an exquisite revelation for me, for I had never had the privilege of receiving flowers before. Hence, it proved to be an exceptionally significant occasion, evoking a profound sense of delight that surpassed my wildest expectations. The arrangement contained a heartfelt note, unequivocally indicating his admiration for me.

Your online acquaintance will exhibit indications of harboring sentiments beyond those of a typical friendship, consistently showering you with compliments or presenting you with gifts. It is evident that you are experiencing great joy. Therefore, during your conversation with him, kindly introduce the notion of potentially convening in person and inquire about his perspective on the matter. It is advisable to ascertain whether he regards you seriously and possesses genuine interest, thus averting potential disillusionment in the future.

We appreciate the experience of being loved and wish to encounter an individual who possesses a comprehensive understanding of our identity. We seek someone who exemplifies honesty and integrity, and we envision the potential for an emotional connection, even acknowledging the potential risk of emotional vulnerability if our affections are unreciprocated. It is imperative to thoroughly acquaint oneself with one's cyber companion and further ascertain the true essence of the individual with whom one is developing profound feelings from afar.

A Love Confession

Gradually, Mark demonstrated his genuine interest in me, albeit without explicit admissions, leaving me uncertain of the sincerity of his affection. I patiently anticipated his initiative to communicate with me and convey his sentiments; however, when I realized that he failed to do so, I resolved to subtly indicate my interest in him. Nevertheless, I pondered over the most appropriate method to accomplish this task.

Articulating emotions on the Internet can prove challenging, particularly when encountering an elusive individual who resides distantly in a foreign country, as was my personal experience. If you choose to undertake the significant decision of expressing your emotions to your online companion, it is imperative that you exercise caution and discernment in your approach. It is advisable to refrain from conveying your affection towards him in a lengthy email of considerable length, as this has the potential to intimidate and alienate your online acquaintance.

On a certain day, I made the decision to transmit a digital greeting card, commonly referred to as an ecard, to Mark. The purpose of this electronic medium was to convey a concise yet unequivocal message: "You consistently occupy my thoughts and reside within my heart." Coincidentally, this exchange took place on the occasion of St. Valentine's Day, and to my delight, Mark responded promptly. He corresponded with me via email, expressing his reciprocation of sentiments, and from that instant onward, we came to ascertain the existence of love within our relationship, thereby transcending the boundaries of mere friendship. Mark expressed that I brought fulfillment to his existence and harbored deeply affectionate sentiments towards me. Consequently, this is how he assumed the role of my cyber companion.

Talking about the Past

In the course of acquainting ourselves with one another as a couple, there shall arise an opportune juncture wherein you may develop an inquisitive nature concerning our respective prior romantic involvements, the openness of which dialogue will hinge upon the presence of mutual trust.

Trust plays a vital role in fostering a successful relationship, gradually building, rooted in mutual respect and unwavering honesty. There exist numerous instances wherein individuals have suffered harm at the hands of their partners, leading them to actively suppress any recollections pertaining to their past experiences. It is conceivable that they might have experienced infidelity or a tumultuous divorce, thus it would be advisable to refrain from pressuring one's cyberboyfriend to discuss these matters. Alternatively, it is also possible that you, as the individual in question, may not yet feel prepared to broach such topics.

When a couple deeply cherishes and values each other, they will identify an opportune occasion to engage in discussions regarding their past and share those intimate narratives that may be challenging to broach openly. Once a strong foundation of trust is established between both individuals, the bond will significantly deepen, facilitating open and uninhibited communication on a broad range of topics.

However, there are also individuals who have an extensive history of relationships in the digital realm. Certain individuals may choose to keep this information concealed, while others are candid about their past experiences of love, providing intricate details about each romantic encounter. Caution must be exercised when encountering an individual actively seeking an online escapade by one's side. The scenario remains unchanged when a woman discusses her numerous previous partners; she will not be regarded seriously by a man seeking a committed relationship.

The internet provides a platform for individuals who have experienced a break up, separation, or divorce to discover a compatible partner. Searching for a suitable companion in the digital sphere entails moving beyond one's past and eagerly anticipating a fresh romantic connection. Every woman deserves contentment and the opportunity to encounter a partner who possesses the aptitude to regard, appreciate, and ardently love them.

Flirting via Chat

As trust is established within the relationship with your online partner, you will find that your interactions become characterized by heightened affection and increased mutual vulnerability. It implies that you will likewise engage in intimate exchanges through chat or email communication.

After Mark openly expressed his sincerest emotions towards me, our relationship progressed further, and he began endearingly referring to me with affectionate terms typically used between romantic partners, such as "My Love" or "My Heart". Romanticism permeates the core of the relationship, leading to the organic expression of affection through subtle flirtation.

A spontaneous exchange of heartfelt dialogue may arise unexpectedly, wherein you discover that you have shared a personal photograph with your online significant other, who responds with compliments on your appearance. Furthermore, they reveal that thoughts of you have been occupying their mind and even manifesting in dreams. He may express to you: I experienced somnolence while contemplating your presence, wherein I envisioned an occurrence wherein I held you close, inhaling the fragrance emanating from your person, gently caressing your exquisitely undulating tresses while your enticing lips entreated me to bestow upon them a tender kiss.

If you encounter such a comment in a chat, it is likely that the individual is expressing romantic interest in you. The decision to further engage in the conversation rests upon you, and you can choose to respond accordingly, perhaps with a response such as:

And may I inquire as to why you did not bestow upon me a stolen kiss in that dream? I would have greatly appreciated if you had done that.

An exchange of words can transition from a romantic discourse to a stimulating and sensual interaction, allowing for the exchange of personal revelations and expressions of intimacy.

Depending on the depth of conversation, one may potentially engage in what is commonly known as Cybersex. Your most profound contemplations and creative capacity have the potential to envision a romantic encounter within the space that separates you and your online significant other.

Seduction in the Distance

Every female is inherently endowed with the ability to captivate others, an innate quality that lies within us. It is a natural attribute, a virtue that we possess and employ when we develop an interest in someone. The majority of males are inclined towards females who possess self-assurance, while maintaining humility. In order to captivate an individual from afar, it is indeed conceivable by exercising prudence in managing the affairs of a person of interest, as well as maintaining meticulousness in one's exchanges via email or online messaging platforms. It is imperative to demonstrate genuine concern towards him and exhibit a sincere curiosity in engaging with the myriad of topics he brings up in conversation.

When it comes to the art of attraction, it is imperative to present oneself in a manner that leaves a profound impression on the counterpart. Each of us possesses a unique charisma, and it is imperative that we make optimal use of it. If you plan to engage in a romantic rendezvous through online communication, it is advisable to prepare oneself as if it were a conventional, in-person encounter. It is recommended to opt for a natural appearance, refraining from concealing one's beautiful hair, regardless of its length. Avoid the use of headwear or hairstyles that cover the hair, and instead showcase it as it naturally is. Additionally, choose attire that exudes a sense of allure, while being mindful not to reveal an excessive amount of skin. It is acceptable to display a modest amount of cleavage, but exercise caution in the extent to which you do so, as presenting an overt amount may convey an unintended impression.

It has been established that men derive enjoyment from engaging in the art of seduction, a mutually satisfying activity that can be pursued through online communication. With a touch of ingenuity, one can create a narrative, be it a tale of romance or a more risqué affair, wherein you and your virtual partner assume the leading roles. Imagine scenes such as strolling hand-in-hand along a moonlit shoreline or finding ourselves trapped in a malfunctioning elevator, with only each other for company. The concept of seduction in this game beckons you to construct a tableau where you may candidly articulate your desires as a couple, envisioning a scenario that will foster intimacy and dispel the distance between you.

There will come a time when you and he will engage in regular daily conversations, regardless of your geographical separation. During these exchanges, you will have the opportunity to share your emotions and experiences, thereby opening up the possibility of developing romantic feelings.

Cybersex

The term Cybersex originates from the notion of engaging in sexual activities through computer-mediated communication. It is an online interaction facilitated through chat and web cam, where individuals in a romantic relationship can openly communicate their intimate desires, arousing sexual fantasies and experiences.

Upon meeting my partner through online means, we engaged in conversational exchanges, albeit without the privilege of utilizing a web camera. In our particular case, we ascertained the definition of Cybersex solely through the utilization of online chat platforms.

If you and your online partner experience sexual attraction, despite the geographical distance between you, it may be feasible to organize intimate encounters via video conferencing. By doing so, you will openly articulate the affectionate emotions harbored by both parties and acknowledge your romantic attraction. In the realm of Cybersex, the exercise of imagination occupies a substantial role. It entails the creation of a fantasy, wherein one assumes a role, thus enabling the indulgence in a virtual sexual encounter.

Engaging in digital intimacy is a feasible prospect that may occur when both parties have developed a genuine rapport, engaged in prolonged communication, and established a foundation of trust with one another. One of you will initiate a conversation in which it becomes apparent that there is a level of attraction towards your online acquaintance. There are various possibilities for such situations to occur. For instance, one could communicate a message to their online romantic partner in the following manner: "

I am deeply desirous of accompanying you while strolling along the shoreline during the night hours, gazing intently into your eyes, and softly imparting to you my profound longing for your presence. To bestow upon you a tender caress upon your neck, followed by another gentle embrace in proximity to your lips. I am unable to conceal the depth of my desire to be in your presence. Your virtual partner is being extended an invitation to partake in your imaginative realm. It will be at the discretion of both individuals involved to relish the experience and maximize its potential.

When there is mutual interest between a man and a woman, the resulting attraction is significantly potent and the inclination to be in each other's company intensifies with time. The physical distance between individuals holds no significance in the realm of chat-based communication, as the awareness of geographical separation becomes inconsequential, thereby allowing for an increase in the frequency of chat interactions between loved ones.

Your Perfect Match

You have been enrolled in an online dating platform with the primary objective of seeking a potential life partner, and eventually, you have fortuitously crossed paths with a truly exceptional individual who shares your specific interests. You had a preexisting friendship that has now developed into a virtual romantic relationship. This signifies a transition from being cyberfriends to becoming cyberboyfriend and girlfriend, indicating a strong compatibility between the two.

Mark and I engaged in written correspondence for a period exceeding six months prior to our initial face-to-face encounter. Our communication primarily involved chat platforms, supplemented by frequent telephone conversations. Our connection transcended mere attraction; we were not mere acquaintances, but rather, we came to the realization that we were deeply in love, sharing mutual sentiments. I was the one who initially proposed the notion of arranging a physical encounter with Mark.

Mark is the gentleman whom I yearned to embark upon a lifelong journey with, an arduous quest concluded by my fortuitous encounter with him. The geographical distance between Mark and myself did not present a hindrance. In mutual assurance, we both maintained a firm belief that our paths would intersect, allowing us to validate our emotions, deliberate over our shared destiny, and discuss our aspirations as partners.

If you have strong conviction regarding your emotions and firmly believe that your cyberboyfriend is the ideal partner for you, while concurrently observing obvious indications that he reciprocates those sentiments, it is appropriate to initiate a discussion regarding a potential initial meeting.

www.ingramcontent.com/pod-product-compliance
Lightning Source LLC
Chambersburg PA
CBHW050232120526
44590CB00016B/2055